# Book 1
## CompTIA A+
### By Solis Tech

# &

# Book 2
## Raspberry Pi 2
### By Solis Tech

# Book 1
## CompTIA A+
**By Solis Tech**

# *All-in-One Certification Exam Guide for Beginners!*

**CompTIA A+:** All-in-One Certification Exam Guide for Beginners!

# Table Of Contents

# Introduction

I want to thank you and congratulate you for purchasing the book, *"CompTIA A+: All-in-One Certification Exam Guide for Beginners!"*

This book contains proven steps and strategies on how to prepare for the CompTIA A+ exams.

This eBook will explain the basics of the CompTIA A+ certification and tests. It will also give you some pointers regarding the topics that you need to review. By reading this book, you will gain the knowledge and skills required to pass the tests.

Thanks again for purchasing this book, I hope you enjoy it!

# Chapter 1: The CompTIA A+ Examination

This eBook is written for people who are knowledgeable about computers. It assumes that you know to how to use a computer and its peripherals (e.g. printers, modems, etc.). This book will serve as your guide in preparing for the CompTIA A+ exam.

### The A+ Certification

This is a certification program developed by CompTIA (Computer Technology Industry Association). This program is designed to provide a consistent way of checking the competency of computer technicians. The A+ certificate is given to people who have reached the degree of knowledge and diagnostic skills required to give proper support in the PC industry.

The A+ certification is similar to other programs in the industry (e.g. Microsoft Certified Systems Engineer and Novell's Certified Novel Engineer). The principle behind these certification programs is that if you need to get services for their products, you want to find technicians who have been certified by these programs.

### The Benefits of Being A+ Certified

There are many reasons to get your own A+ certification. The information packet distributed by CompTIA gives the following benefits:

- It serves as a proof of your professional achievement.

- It improves your marketability.

- It gives you excellent advancement opportunities.

- It is now considered as a requirement for other kinds of advanced computer training.

- It encourages customers to do business with you

### How to Become Certified

The A+ certification is given to anyone who passes the exams. You are not required to work for any company. CompTIA is not a secret group or society. It is, on the other hand, a group of elite computer technicians. If you want to be A+ certified, you have to do these things:

- Pass the exam called A+ Essentials

- Pass one of the three technician examinations:

- o IT Technician Test

- o Depot Technician Test

- o Remote Support Technician Test

You can take the tests at any Pearson VUE or Thompson Prometric testing center. If you will pass both exams, you will receive a mail from CompTIA. That letter will inform you that you passed the tests. Additionally, it contains the certificate, a lapel pin, and a business card.

### *How to Sign Up for the Exams*

To sign up for the tests, you may call Pearson VUE at 1-877-551-7587 or register online at www.vue.com. For Thompson Prometric, call 1-800-777-4276 or visit the website www.2test.com.

These companies will ask for your name, employer, phone number, mailing address, and SSN (Social Security Number). If you don't want to give out your SSN, a provisional number will be given to you. Additionally, they will ask when and where you want to take the exam.

Obviously, the exams aren't free. You have to pay your chosen testing company. That means you have to specify the payment arrangement during the registration process. You can simply provide your credit card information to the customer representative you will talk to. If you're doing it online, you can enter the credit card info on their payment page.

### *Who Should Use This Book?*

If you want to pass the A+ tests, and do it confidently, you should use this book as a guide for your preparations. The A+ Essentials test is created to measure basic skills for an entry-level computer technician. The technician tests are designed to certify that you have the required skills to service microcomputer hardware.

This eBook was created with one purpose in mind: to help you pass the A+ exams. This guide will do that by explaining the things on which you will be tested.

# Chapter 2: The Different Parts of a Computer

A PC (i.e. personal computer) is a machine made up of different components that work together to perform tasks (e.g. helping you write a document or add up large numbers). With this definition, notice that computers are described as having various distinct parts that work together harmoniously. Nowadays, almost all computers are modular. That is, they possess parts that can be replaced if the owner wants to improve the performance of his device. Each part has a specific purpose. In this chapter, you'll learn about the parts that make up a common PC, how they work, and what their functions are.

Important Note: Unless stated otherwise, the terms "computer" and "PC" can be used interchangeably throughout this eBook.

### *The Different Parts of a Motherboard*

The motherboard, also called the system or planar board, serves as the "spine" of a PC. This is the brown or green circuit board that you'll find at the bottom of your computer. The system board is the most important part of a PC since it houses and/or connects the other parts of a computer together.

#### Different Types of Motherboards

There are two main types of motherboards. These are:

*Integrated Motherboards* – With this type, most of the parts are integrated into the system board's circuitry. Basically, integrated motherboards are created for simplicity. Since majority of the components are already part of the board itself, you won't have to install them individually. However, this simplicity has a major drawback: once a component stops working, you cannot simply replace it; you have to replace the entire motherboard. These boards are cheap to manufacture but expensive to repair.

Note: If one of the parts breaks, you may just disable it and add an expansion card that has similar capabilities.

*Nonintegrated Motherboards* – Here, the major parts (e.g. disk controllers, video circuitry, etc.) are installed as expansion cards. You will easily identify this kind of system board since every expansion slot is occupied by a major component.

#### The Different Form Factors of Motherboards

Computer experts also classify motherboards according to their design (also known as *form factor*). Here are the main form factors being used today: NLX, BTX, ATX, and micro ATX. You have to be vigilant when buying a computer case and system board separately. Some cases lack flexibility: they might not accommodate the system board you will select.

Let's discuss each form factor:

1.  NLX – This is the abbreviation for "New Low-profile Extended". In general, this form factor is used for cases that are low-profile. With this design, the expansion slots (e.g. PCI, ISA, etc.) are placed on a special card to reduce the vertical space they occupy. Daughter boards, or adapter cards, that are normally plugged vertically into the expansion slots, are placed parallel to the system board. That means their size won't affect that of the computer case.

2.  BTX – This form factor was launched by Intel back in 2003. With this design, the head-producing parts are lined up against the power supply's exhaust fan and the air intake vents. Then, the other components are cooled by installing heat sinks on the motherboard. This design offers a quiet setup since it involves efficient airflow paths and fewer exhaust fans.

3.  ATX – With ATX motherboards, the processor and memory slots form a 90° angle with the expansion cards. This design places the memory and processor in line with the power supply's exhaust fan. Thus, the processor can remain cool while it runs. In addition, you may add expansion cards (even the full-length ones) to an ATX motherboard since the memory and processor are not parallel to the expansion cards.

4.  Micro ATX – This form factor is similar with the previous one, with one major difference: it is designed for smaller computer cases. Micro ATX motherboards benefit from the enhanced cooling designs of their full-sized counterparts. However, since they are smaller, they have lesser motherboard headers, integrated components, expansion slots, and memory modules.

### *Processors – Their Functions and Characteristics*

Now that you are familiar with system boards, you have to learn about their most important part: the central processing unit (CPU). The CPU controls all of the computer's activities using both internal and external buses. Basically, it is a processor chip that contains millions of transistors.

**Important Note**: Nowadays, the word "chip" describes the whole package that a computer technician may install into a socket. However, this word was originally used to refer to the silicon wafer hidden inside the carrier (i.e. the "chip" you see on your motherboard). The pins that you see on the outer part of the carrier are connected to the silicon wafer's small contacts. These pins allow you to install the carrier into a socket.

You can identify which part inside the PC is the central processing unit: the CPU is a large square that lies flat on the motherboard with a large fan and heat sink.

### The Features of Modern Processors

- Hyperthreading – This word refers to HTT (hyper-threading technology). Basically, HTT is a variant of SMT (simultaneous multithreading). This kind of technology uses the scalar architecture of modern CPUs.

  HTT-capable CPUs appear as two different processors to the computer's operating system (OS). Because of this, the OS may assign two processes simultaneously, such as symmetric multi-processing, where multiple processors utilize the same network resources. Actually, the OS should support SMP in order to use HTT. If a process fails because of missing information caused by, for instance, branch prediction problems, the processor's execution resources can be reassigned for a different procedure that can be conducted immediately. Thus, the processor's downtime is dramatically reduced.

- Multicore – A CPU that has a multicore design contains two processors inside the same package. Here, the OS may treat the CPU as if it were two different CPUs. Just like the HTT, the OS should support SMP. Additionally, SMP is not considered as an upgrade if the apps run on the SMP system are not meant for parallel processes. A good example for the multicore technology is the i7 Quad-Core Processor from Intel.

- Microcode – This is the group of instructions (also called instruction set) that compose the different microprograms that the CPU executes as it performs its functions. The MMX (multimedia extensions) is a special example of an individual microprogram that performs a specific instruction set. Basically, microcodes are at a lower level than the codes used in computer programs. On average, each instruction from a computer program requires a large number of microinstructions. Intel and other processor manufacturers incorporate the MMX instruction set into their products.

- Overclocking – This feature allows you to increase the performance of your CPU, on par with processors created to function at overclocked rates. However, unlike processors created to function on that speed, you have to make sure that the overclocked processor doesn't damage itself from the increased level of heat. You might need to install an advanced cooling system (e.g. liquid cooling) to protect the CPU and other computer parts.

- Throttling – Processor throttling, also called clamping, is the process that specifies the CPU time to be spent on a computer program. By specifying how individual programs use the processor, you can "treat" all of the applications fairly. The principle of Application Fairness turns into a major problem for servers, where each program may represent the work of another user. That means fairness to computer programs becomes fairness to the users (i.e. the actual customers). Customers of modern terminal servers take advantage of this feature.

## Memory – Its Functions and Characteristics

Nowadays, memory is one of the easy, popular, and inexpensive methods to enhance a computer. While the computer's processor runs, it stores data in the machine's memory. Basically, the more memory a machine has, the faster it can operate.

To determine the memory of a computer, search for thin sets of small circuit boards that are packed together near the CPU. These circuit boards sit vertically on the computer's motherboard.

### How to Check for Errors in a Computer's Memory

#### Parity Checking

This is a basic scheme used to check for errors. It lines up the computer chips in a single column and separates them into equal bit groups. These bits are numbered beginning at zero. All of the number $x$ bits, one from every chip, create a numerical array. If you are using "even parity", for instance, you will count up the number of bits contained in the array. If the total number is even, you will set the parity bit to zero since the bit count is already even. If the total is an odd number, on the other hand, you should set the parity bit to 1 in order to even up the bit count.

This technique is effective in identifying the existence of errors in the arrays of bits. However, it cannot indicate the location of the errors and how to solve them. Keep in mind that this isn't error correction – it is just a simple error check.

#### ECC

ECC stands for *Error Checking and Correcting*. If the computer's memory supports this method, the system will generate and store check bits. Whenever the machine accesses its memory, an algorithm will be performed on the check bits. If the result turns out to be zero (or a group of zeros), the information contained in the memory is considered valid and the computer functions as normal. ECC can identify single-bit and double-bit errors. However, it can only correct errors that are single-bit in nature.

### The Four Main Types of Memory

- DRAM – This is perhaps the most popular type of RAM out there. DRAM stands for *Dynamic Random Access Memory*. Because of their inherent simplicity, these memory chips are cheap and easy to create compared to the other types. This kind of memory is called dynamic since it needs constant update signals in order to keep storing the data written there. If the DRAM chips won't receive stable signals, the information they hold will be deleted.

- SRAM – This stands for *Static Random Access Memory*. Unlike DRAMs, this kind of memory doesn't require a steady stream of signals. In general, SRAM chips are more complex and expensive than DRAMs. You can use SRAM for cache functions.

- ROM – This is the abbreviation for Read-Only Memory. It is called as such because it prevents the user from editing the memory it contains. Once the data is written on the computer's ROM, it cannot be changed anymore. ROM is usually used to hold the machine's BIOS, since this data is rarely modified.

- CMOS – This is a special type of memory chip. It is designed to hold the configuration settings of a computer's BIOS. CMOS is battery-powered: that means the configuration is retained even if the machine is turned off.

### Storage Devices – Their Functions and Characteristics

Computers are useless if they can't store anything. Storage devices hold the information being used, as well as the programs and files the computer needs in order to function properly. In general, storage devices are classified according to their capacity, access time, and physical attributes.

### HDD Systems

HDD stands for *Hard Disk Drive*. This storage device is also called hard disk or hard drive. Computers use HDDs to allow quick access to data as well as permanent storage. Typically, hard disks are found inside a computer.

An HDD system is composed of:

Controller – This component controls the storage. It knows how the drive functions, emits signals to the different motors inside the disk, and accepts signals from the sensors within the drive. Nowadays, hard disk manufacturers place the drive and controller in one enclosure.

Hard Disk – This acts as the physical warehouse for the data. HDD systems store data on little disks (about 3-5 inches in diameter) grouped together and kept inside an enclosure.

Host Adapter – This is the system's translator: it converts signals from the controller and hard disk to signals the computer can work with. Most modern motherboards have a built-in host adapter, allowing drive cable connection through board headers.

### *Floppy Drives*

Floppy disks are magnetic storage devices that use plastic diskettes enclosed in a tough casing. Several years ago, floppy disks were used to easily transfer information from one computer to another. Nowadays, few people are using floppy disks because of their small capacity. DVD-ROMs and CD-ROMs have replaced floppy disks in storing and transferring digital information.

### *CD-ROM Drives*

Modern computers use CD-ROM drives. These compact disks are virtually similar to those used in music recording. CD-ROMs allow you to store data for a long period of time. In general, these drives are read-only: you cannot erase or delete the data once it is stored on a CD. In addition, computers need to spend a longer time in "reading" CDs compared to internal hard drives. Why are these drives so popular?

Despite their drawbacks, CD-ROMs are used because they can store large files (about 650MB) and are extremely portable.

### *DVD-ROM Drives*

This is the newest storage device to be used for computers. The DVD (i.e. digital video disc) technology is mostly used for entertainment purposes (e.g. home theater systems). DVD-ROMs are basically similar to the DVDs you use at home. Because of this, computers that are equipped with a DVD-ROM drive can play movies stored on a DVD.

However, DVD-ROMs are way much more useful when used for computers. Since they use newer technology, DVD-ROMs are better than CD-ROMs in terms of storage capacity. On average, DVDs can hold 4GB of data. That means DVD-ROMs are your best option if you are storing or distributing large files.

Important Note: CD-ROMs and DVD-ROMs have the same appearance. The single difference is the logo on the front of DVD drives.

### *Removable Storage Devices*

Many years ago, the term "removable storage" meant something extremely different from what it means now. Tape backup is one of the old storage devices that can still be bought today. Modern computer users prefer the solid-state, random-access removable storage devices. In this section, you'll learn about tape backups and the new storage solutions.

### _Tape Backup_

This is an old type of removable storage. A tape backup device can be installed externally or internally and utilize either an analog or digital magnetic tape to store data. In general, this kind of device can hold more information than other storage mediums. However, they are also one of the slowest in terms of data transfer rate. Because of these reasons, tape backup devices are mainly used for archived information.

### _Flash Memory_

Before, random-access memory chips were only used to access and use data. But now, you'll find them in different physical sizes and storage capacities. Flash memory drives are considered as the best solid-state storage device available. The flash memory category includes SD (secure digital) and other memory cards, USB flash drives, and older detachable and non-detachable memory mechanisms. Each of these storage devices has the capability to store huge amounts of information.

Manufacturers of flash memory devices use revolutionary packaging (e.g. keychain attachments) for their products to provide easy transport options for their end-users.

# Chapter 3: How to Work With Computer Parts Effectively

While taking the CompTIA A+ exam, you will answer questions regarding the installation, usage, and replacement of computer parts. This chapter will help you to review regarding those topics.

### *How to Install, Configure and Optimize Computer Parts*

Aside from knowing the characteristics and functions of PC components, you also need to know how to use them. In particular, you should be familiar with the installation, configuration, and optimization of such parts.

#### *How to Upgrade a Storage Device*

Storage devices are available in different shapes and sizes. Aside from IDE and SCSI, two of the most popular types, there are SATA (Serial ATA) and PATA (Parallel ATA). You can also     differentiate between external and internal drives. This section of the book will explain each of these options.

#### Preparing the Drive

Regardless of the technology being used, you should format storage devices before using them. Although most drives have their own formatting software, each OS has a tool that you can use. When working with Windows computers, you can utilize the format utility through the command line. If you are working with XP, Vista, 7, or newer Windows system, you can also use the graphical utility program called Disk Management.

#### How to Work with IDE

Before, IDE (integrated drive electronics) drives were the most popular kind of computer hard drives. Although they are often linked to hard drives, IDE is more than just an interface for hard disks. It can also serve as the interface for different storage types such as Zip, DVD, and CD-ROM.

To install IDE drives, you should:

1. Set the slave/master jumper on the IDE drive.

2. Place the drive inside the drive bay.

3. Connect the cable for power-supply.

4. Link the ribbon cable to the motherboard and to the drive.

5. If the drive isn't detected automatically, you should configure it using the BIOS Setup of your computer.

6. Use your PC's operating system to format and partition the IDE drive.

## How to Work with SCSI

SCSI is the abbreviation for *Small Computer System Interface*. This kind of device can be either external or internal to the machine. To configure an SCSI device, you should assign an SCSI ID (also called SCSI address) to all of the devices in the SCSI bus. You can configure their numbers using a jumper or DIP switch.

Whenever the computer sends data to the SCSI device, it emits a signal on the cable assigned to that number. The device will respond with a signal that holds the device's number and the information needed.

You should install a terminator (i.e. terminating resistor device) at the two ends of the bus to keep the SCSI devices working. You can activate and/or deactivate terminators using a jumper.

Here are the things you should do when installing an SCSI device:

- For Internal Devices – Connect the cable (i.e. a 50-wire ribbon cable with multiple keyed connectors) to the adapter and to each SCSI device in your computer. Afterward, place the terminators on the adapter and terminate the final device in the chain. You should leave other devices unterminated.

- For External Devices - Follow the steps outlined above, but here, you should use some stub cables between the SCSI devices in the daisy chain (instead of a long cable that has multiple connectors). Terminate the adapter as well as the final device in the daisy chain (that device should have one stub cable linked to it).

- For Hybrid Devices – Many types of adapters have connectors for external and internal SCSI devices. If you have this kind of adapter, attach the ribbon cable to your internal devices and connect the cable to your adapter. Afterward, daisy-chain the external devices from the external port. Terminate the device at the end of every chain. Make sure that the adapter is unterminated.

### *External Storage Devices*

As capacities shoot up and prices fall down, the number of available external storage devices has increased greatly. Aside from the SCSI variant explained above, you will also see devices with USB connections and those that can connect straight to the system. The computer's operating system will recognize USB devices upon connection. You can just install any additional programs you like to use. A computer program called Dantz Retrospect is included in many storage devices to allow you to utilize external devices as automatic backups.

If the external storage device is linked straight to the system, you can just follow the instructions that came with that product. Then, install additional programs on the computers that you will be using. The main benefit of linking straight to the system is that the storage device/s can be accessed by all of the computers.

### How to Upgrade Display Devices

Before linking or unlinking a display device (e.g. a computer monitor), make sure that the computer and the device itself are powered off. Afterward, connect a cable from the computer's video card to the display device. Connect the power cord of that device to an electrical outlet. You may use a modern Digital Visual Interface (DVI) cable or the traditional DB-15 (or VGA) cable.

While installing a new monitor, you should have the proper driver. The driver is the software interface between the display device and the computer's OS. If you don't have the right driver, your monitor won't display what you want to see. Nowadays, you can download the newest drivers from the website of monitor manufacturers.

Aside from the power supply, the most dangerous part to repair is the monitor. Computer technicians say that beginners should never attempt to repair monitors. Monitors can hold high-voltage charges even if they have been powered off for several hours. That means you can be electrocuted if you will try to repair a monitor by yourself. If your monitor stopped working, and you don't want to buy a new one, you should take that device to a TV repair shop or a certified computer technician. The technicians and the repair guys know how to fix monitors properly – they understand the dangers and the correct procedures.

### How to upgrade Input and Multimedia Devices

The typical upgrade for input devices is the transition to newer mice and keyboards.

#### Keyboards

Keyboards may wear out if used repeatedly. The usual problem is "key sticking", where keys are no longer responding to the user. To replace a PS/2 101-key keyboard with a new one, just unplug the old keyboard and plug in the new. As you can see, this is a quick and easy process. Nowadays, however, computer users prefer to replace old keyboards with USB ones.

Here is a principle you need to remember: You can use the "unplug-the-old-and-plug-in-the-new" procedure as long as your computer's OS supports the keyboard you want to use.

#### Mice

17

Computer mice also wear out because of repeated use. But don't worry: you can replace old mice with new ones. You may easily replace a PS/2 connection mouse with another without spending too much. As an alternative, you may buy an optical mouse (which prevents dust- and ball-related problems) or a wireless one (which needs batteries to send and receive signals). Although new mouse models still use the PS/2 type of connection, most mouse products in the market use the USB connection.

# Chapter 4: The Tools Needed for Checking Computer Parts

The CompTIA A+ exam will also test your skills in checking computer parts. This chapter will help you with that topic by discussing the tools and diagnostic procedures needed.

### *The Tools Needed by a Computer Technician*

A great computer technician needs a great collection of tools. If you are working alone, you may not get past the troubleshooting phase. However, you still need to use certain tools in order to succeed in that task. Once you have identified the problem, you will need to get another set of tools in order to fix it.

This book will focus on the "hardware" tools. These are:

- Screwdrivers – When checking a computer technician's toolkit, you will surely find screwdrivers. Almost all of the big computer parts you'll see today are mounted using screws. If you need to remove these parts, you need to have the right type of screwdriver. This kind of tool is divided into three types:

    o Flat-Blade – Many people refer to this as the *common* or *standard* screwdriver. The screw used with this screwdriver is rarely used today (mainly because the screw's head can be destroyed easily).

    o Phillips – This is perhaps the most popular type of screwdrivers being used today. The screws used with a Phillips screwdriver have enough head surface: you can turn them many times without damaging the screws' head. According to recent reports, more than 90% of the screws used in computers belong to the Phillips-head type.

    o Torx – This is the type of screwdriver you use while working on tiny screws found on Apple and Compaq computers. The screws you remove using a Torx screwdriver have the most surface to work against: they offer the best resistance in terms of screw-head damage. Nowadays, Torx-type screws are gaining more popularity because of their clean and technical look.

- Flashlight – This is one of the tools you should always have. You'll realize how important this tool is when you're crawling under a table searching for a dropped computer part.

- Needle-Nose Pliers – You should have this in your toolkit. This kind of pliers is great for holding connectors or tiny screws (particularly if you have large hands). If needle-nose pliers are still too big to do certain tasks, you may use a pair of tweezers.

- Compressed Air – While working on a computer, you will usually remove the machine's case first. Once the cover is removed, it would be great if you will clean the computer's internal components. The clumps of dirt and fibers can block airflow inside the system unit. As a result, the PC's life will be shortened. The ideal way to eliminate the dust is by using compressed air.

  If you are working for a big company, you probably have a core air compressor that supplies compressed air. If this kind of compressor is not available, you may purchase canned compressed air. However, you'll be shelling out large amounts of money – cans of compressed air are expensive.

- Soldering Iron – You can use it to splice broken wires. Nowadays, computer technicians rarely use this tool. Here's the reason: modern computer parts are created with quick-disconnect connectors. You can easily replace them without splicing anything.

- Wire Strippers – Whenever you have to solder something, you need to use a stripper/wire cutter to prepare the wires for connection. Stripping means you will expose a certain part of the wire by removing the insulation.

- Multi-Meters – This tool is named as such because it is basically a set of different types of testing meters, such as ammeter, voltmeter, and ohmmeter. When used by a trained technician, a multi-meter can identify the failure of various types of computer parts.

  A multi-meter has an analog or digital display, a mode selector switch, and two probes. You can use the switch to perform two things: (1) select the function you want to test and (2) choose the range in which the meter will work. If you need to use an old meter to measure a power pack, you should manually set the range selector. Modern multi-meters, particularly the digital ones, can automatically find the correct ranges.

  Important Note: You should never measure voltage by connecting a manual ranging multi-meter to an AC electrical outlet. This will damage the meter itself, the meter mechanisms, or both.

How to Measure Resistance Using a Multi-Meter

Resistance is the property of electricity commonly measured when troubleshooting computer parts. This electrical property is measured in ohms and represented by the Greek letter "omega." If a multi-meter indicates infinite resistance, the electric currents cannot travel from one prove to another. If you are using a multi-meter to check the resistance and you are getting an infinite reading, there's a huge possibility that the wire is broken.

When measuring resistance, you should set the tool to measure ohms. You can do it using either the selector dial or the front button. Then, connect the PC component you want to measure between the tool's probes. The multi-meter will then show the component's resistance value.

### How to Measure Voltage Using a Multi-Meter

This process is similar to the one discussed above, but with two main differences:

1. While measuring voltage, make sure that you properly connect each probe to the source of electricity. For DC voltage, the "-" should be connected to the negative side and the "+" to the positive one. This positioning is irrelevant when measuring AC voltage.

2. You should switch the selector to Volts DC (VDC) or Volts AC (VAC), depending on what you need to measure, to instruct the tool about the voltage you are working with. These settings protect the tool from overload. The multi-meter will blow up if you will plug it into a power source while it's still on "measure resistance" mode.

# Chapter 5: Operating Systems

The CompTIA A+ examination will test your knowledge regarding operating systems. Since operating systems play an important role in the computer industry, you should be familiar with them. This chapter will guide you in this topic. Here, you'll learn different things about a computer's OS.

### *What is an Operating System?*

Computers are useless if they don't have any piece of software. Well, you can use them as a doorstop or paperweight – but that is not cost-efficient. You need to have an interface before you can use the capabilities of a computer. And, if you don't know yet, software acts as the interface. Although there are different kinds of software, or computer programs, the most important one you'll ever need is the OS.

Operating systems have various functions, most of which are extremely complex. However, two functions are critical:

1. Interfacing with the computer's hardware

2. Providing an environment in which other pieces of software can run.

Here are the three main types of software that you will encounter in the CompTIA exam:

- Operating System – It provides a stable environment for other computer programs. In addition, it allows the user to enter and execute commands. The operating system gives the user an interface so they can enter commands (i.e. input) and get results or feedback (i.e. output). For this, the OS should communicate with the PC's hardware and conduct the tasks below:

    o   Device access

    o   Output format

    o   Memory management

    o   File and disk management

Once the operating system has performed these basic tasks, the user can enter instructions to the computer using an input device (e.g. a mouse or keyboard). Some of the commands are pre-installed in the operating system, whereas others are given using certain applications. The OS serves as the platform on which the PC's hardware, other pieces of software, and the user work together.

- Application – This is used to complete a specific task. Basically, an application is a computer program written to support the commands given to the OS. Every application is compiled or configured for the operating system it will be used for. Because of this, the application depends on the OS to perform most of its basic functions.

  When a program accesses the computer's memory and linked devices, it sends a request to the OS. The machine's operating system will perform the requests made by the program being used. This setup helps greatly in decreasing the programming overhead, since most of the executable codes are shared – they are written onto the operating system and can be used by different applications installed on the computer.

- Driver – This is an extremely specific program created to instruct an operating system on how to access and use a piece of hardware (e.g. webcam, flash memory, etc.). Every webcam or flash memory has distinct features and settings – the driver helps the OS in knowing how the new hardware works and the things it can do.

### *The Terms and Concepts Related to Operating Systems*

In this section, let's define some of the most important terms and concepts. Study this section carefully since it will teach you the terms you'll encounter during the CompTIA A+ exam.

#### *Key Terms*

- Source – This is the code that explains how computer programs work. An operating system can be open source or closed source.

  o Open Source – The users have the right to change and examine the code.

  o Closed Source – The users are not allowed to edit or check the code.

- Version – This is a specific variant of a computer program, usually expressed by a number, which informs users regarding the "newness" of the software. For instance, MS-DOS is now in its sixth main version. Computer programmers distinguish minor revisions from major ones this way:

  o "Program" 4.0 to "Program" 5.0 is a major revision.

  o "Program" 5.0 to "Program" 5.2 is a minor revision.

- Shell – A piece of software that works on top of the operating system. It allows users to execute commands through an array of menus or a different type of graphical interface. A shell makes an operating system simpler and easier to use by modifying the GUI (graphical user interface).

- GUI – The method by which a user communicates with computers. A GUI uses a touchpad, mouse, or a different mechanism (aside from a keyboard) to interact with the machine and issue commands.

- Multithreading – The capability of a computer program to contain several requests in the computer's CPU. Since it allows an application to perform different tasks simultaneously, computers experience a boost in performance and efficiency.

- Network – A group of computers that are connected by a communication link. A network allows computers to share resources and information.

- Preemptive Multitasking – This is a multitasking technique in which the operating system allocates each program a certain amount of CPU time. Afterward, the OS takes back the control and provides another task or program access to the CPU. Basically, if a computer program crashes, the operating system takes the processor from the faulty program and gives it to the next one (which must be working). Even though unstable computer programs still get locked, only the affected application will stop – not the whole machine.

- Cooperative Multitasking – This is a multitasking technique that relies on the applications themselves. Here, each program is responsible for utilizing and giving up access to the CPU. Windows 3.1 used this method to manage multiple programs. If an application stalls while it is using the CPU, the application fails to free the CPU properly, and the whole computer gets locked, the user needs to reboot the machine.

# Conclusion

Thank you again for purchasing this book!

I hope this book was able to help you to prepare for the CompTIA A+ tests.

The next step is to reread this book and use other information sources. That way, you can increase your chances of passing the exam.

Finally, if you enjoyed this book, please take the time to share your thoughts and post a review on Amazon. It'd be greatly appreciated!

Thank you and good luck!

# Book 2
# Raspberry Pi 2
### By Solis Tech

# Raspberry Pi 2 Programming Made Easy!

**Raspberry Pi 2:** Raspberry Pi 2 Programming Made Easy!

## Table of Contents

# Introduction

Greetings. Thank you for purchasing this book Raspberry Pi 2: Raspberry Pi 2 Programming Made Easy. If you're reading this book then most likely you are here to learn about his nifty new little computer called the Raspberry Pi. In this book, we'll teach you everything that you need to know to get up and running with this little, but powerful computer.

We'll teach you about its parts, its specifications, setting up the operating system, its capabilities and limitations, and ultimately how to do basic programming. We'll discuss the best programming language that works best with the Raspberry Pi and create your first program with it. Without further ado, let's start your Raspberry Pi journey.

## *Chapter 1: Raspberry Pi – The Basics*

### What is a Raspberry Pi?

So what is it exactly? We'll it's a small credit-card sized single board computer that is intended to help people learn more about programming, how the computer works, etc. The CPU or Central Processing Unit is basically a system-on-a-chip. What that means is it pairs an ARM processor that is used by a lot of embedded systems and cellular phones with a Broadcom GPU (Graphics Processing Unit), which is a fairly powerful graphics processor that's capable of displaying full resolution 1080p HD video.

The amount of RAM (Random Access Memory) that the Raspberry Pi 2 has is 1 Gigabyte. Its previous iteration, the Raspberry Pi 1 Model A+ and Raspberry Pi 1 Model B has 256MB and 512MB RAM respectively. The RAM is shared by both the CPU and the GPU.

The Raspberry Pi 2 starts at $39.00 and that includes just the board. On the board there are 4 USB ports, 40 General Purpose Input/Output (GPIO) pins, a full 1080p HDMI port, a Network/Ethernet port, a 3.5mm audio and composite video jack, a Raspberry Pi (CSI) Camera interface, a Video (DSI) Display interface, a Micro SD card slot, and a VideoCore 3D graphics core. The GPIO is basically for more advanced users who are going to be adding Arduino accessory boards, ribbon cables for communication with other hardware devices, and major electronics projects; robotics, sensors, etc.

### Why Is it Cool to Have a Raspberry Pi?

Most people think the Raspberry Pi is cool because it's a fairly complete computer, it runs on very little power, it's small, and it will not burn a hole through your wallet; it's $39.00, which is less than the cost that you would pay for a dinner with a friend or a loved one. The Raspberry Pi also helps people that are new to computer hardware get into it and get their hands dirty without the cost and risk associated with more expensive standard hardware.

Another thing that's cool about it is that the Graphics Processing Unit is pretty powerful. It can play 1080p HD video, which makes it really attractive to a lot of people as a Media Center PC. In fact, most people buy the Raspberry Pi 2 for that specific reason because it is a cheap multimedia PC.

## What Can You Do With a Raspberry Pi?

So what can you do with this thing? Well, just like what was previously mentioned, if you're really new to computer hardware, the Pi can help you learn about those individual components of most modern computers. And if you want to learn how to do programming, the Raspbian operating system that comes with the Raspberry Pi 2 comes with a lot of tools for programming to help you get started.

So you might be asking, why wouldn't you start learning how to program with the computer that you already have? Well, you can. And that's perfectly fine. However, you can think of the Raspberry Pi as your little playground and your test computer that you don't have to worry about breaking if you screw something up. Even if you do break it, you'll only be losing $39.00.

But if you don't care about all that and you don't care about programming or about learning the hardware and so forth, the Raspberry Pi 2 also makes a really great little Media PC. You can get a small case for it, hook it up to the network, install another operating system that's based on Linux called OpenELEC, which is basically a back-end for XBMC (Xbox Media Center), plug it into your TV, and you're ready to start streaming video and audio content on your high-definition TV.

## *Chapter 2: Hardware Accessories*

In this chapter, we're going to talk about some of the hardware and accessories that you're going to need to get started with the Raspberry Pi 2. First, let's start out with the bare necessities. The two things that you'll definitely need are power and an SD card.

### Power Requirement

Let's take a moment here and talk about power because it's important. The Raspberry Pi is a little picky about its power source. Learning about what you need here for power could save you a lot of headache later down the road. The Raspberry Pi needs 5 volts. That should be anywhere between 4.75 volts minimum and a maximum of 5.25 volts. It should be at least 700 mAh, but the recommended is 1000 mAh.

The reason for the 1000 mAh recommended power is because when you start plugging in a keyboard, mouse, network cable, and other peripherals, these all pull power away from the system. This is also why some Raspberry Pi 2 users say that 1500 mAh to 2000 mAh is even better. Of course, if you're only doing projects close to your desktop computer and you don't really plan to run the Raspberry Pi 24/7, you could just run it off of your desktop system's power with just a USB cable if you want.

### SD Card Storage

There is not on-board storage on the Raspberry Pi. So you need an SD card to run the operating system from and also to store any files. Get at least the Class 4 SD storage. It is recommended that you get the Class 6 or Class 10 if you don't mind spending a little bit more.

However, if it's not available, just get the best one that you can. The cost difference honestly isn't that much, and SD cards are getting cheaper all the time. You'll also need a card reader to transfer the operating system image that you're going to download off of Raspberry Pi's website from your desktop computer to the SD card. You can also buy SD cards with the operating system pre-installed from whosoever your Raspberry Pi vendor is if ever you want to skip the operating system installation on the Pi.

If you want to try out multiple operating systems, you can do that with a single card. However, just keep in mind that you'll overwrite any of your settings that you've played around with in the operating system.

## Interacting With the Raspberry Pi

You'll need to decide on how you want to interact with your Raspberry Pi. You can either do it headless over a network, with a keyboard, mouse and monitor, or you can do a combination of both. For network access, you're going to need a network cable; either a CAT5e or CAT6 to connect to your router. There's also a USB WiFi option, which allows you to connect to your router wirelessly.

If you're going headless, you don't really need a USB keyboard and mouse. They are both optional. It just depends on what you want to use the Raspberry Pi for. Just like what was previously mentioned, if you don't want to use the desktop interface, you can skip using a mouse and just plug in a keyboard. If you're using it as a media center and navigate XBMC, a wireless Bluetooth keyboard is a fantastic option if you want to sit on your couch and navigate your media center.

If you're only planning to login remotely using SSH, you can skip the keyboard entirely, or if you want you can just borrow a keyboard and mouse from another machine for the initial setup before you actually go headless over the network. Raspberry Pi should automatically get an IP address from your router. After your router gives an IP address to your Pi, you can just log in to your router to see the exact IP address that was assigned. You can then connect via SSH using that IP address.

If you don't want to find out what the exact IP address is via the router and instead want to find it out locally, you can pull up the command terminal in Raspbian OS and execute an "ifconfig" command. You can then unplugged your peripherals and go headless from there.

## Displays

Moving on to displays, if your TV or monitor has an HDMI input, that's great because all you'll need to get is a cheap HDMI cable. If your monitor only has DVI-in, you'll need an HDMI to DVI cable or an adapter. Just keep in mind that if you do that, the audio signal that's coming out of the HDMI port will be ignored when you're using a DVI converter.

Depending on your setup, you can use external speakers or a splitter. If you're going to go headless, you can skip purchasing a separate monitor specifically for your Pi and just borrow one for the initial setup if you want to. Otherwise, you can still do most of the setup across the network if you are connected via SSH.

## Raspberry Pi Casing

Moving forward, even though it may look cool keeping your bare board out with a bunch of wires just hanging off, it is probably not the safest thing to do for your Raspberry Pi. So it is recommended that you get a case for your Pi. You can get a prefab case for as little as $5.00. It is completely optional but it does help protect the board. A number of people have made some pretty cool custom cases, all of which are available for purchase on-line.

## *Chapter 3: Installing the Operating System In Your SD Card*

In this chapter we're going to be looking at operating system options and how to actually install it in your Raspberry Pi. First off, you're going to need to consider what your goal is for your Raspberry Pi. Is this going to be a learning or tinkering board? Are you going to be programming or do you just want a quick and cheap home theater PC? For a more general purpose operating system or for the tinkerer and programmer, most people recommend going for Raspbian OS.

The latest version of Raspbian at the time of this writing is Raspbian Jessie Kernel Version 4.1, which was released in November 2015. For a home theater PC, most people recommend getting either OpenELEC or RaspBMC. If you're just not sure and you want to try multiple operating system versions, get two or three SD cards and you can just install a different operating system on each of them. You can swap them out depending on what you feel like doing with your Raspberry Pi. Below is the link where you can download the various operating systems for your Pi:

https://www.raspberrypi.org/downloads/

The Operating system installation method that we're about to discuss is mainly for those who have a Mac or a Linux desktop. If you have Windows, the concept is still pretty much the same. You'll just use a different program to get the disk image onto your SD card with Windows.

**Step 1**

Regardless of which type of PC you're using, you're going to need to download the disk image or images of your preferred operating system for your Raspberry Pi. These are by no means the only options, just the ones that the Raspberry Pi community recommends in order to get you started. The first one, as we've mentioned before, is Raspbian.

There's also another version that came out called Occidentalis, which is actually based on Raspbian but has a more educational slant to it and includes a lot more educational tools. For a home theater PC, you'll want to install either OpenELEC or RaspBMC. Both of these are built around the XBMC (Xbox Media Center).

## Step 2

Once you have chosen your operating system, click the download link and choose a location in your computer that you're going to easily remember. Once your download is complete, it would probably be in a .zip file format so you'll need to unzip it and you should now have an image file with an .img file extension. There are a lot of different methods to get this image onto the SD card, but if you're on Linux or Mac, we're just going to use the "dd" command to write the image on the card.

We're going with this method mainly because it's installed in almost every UNIX-based system and it should work pretty much the same on all of them. Before we proceed in talking about DD in Mac or Linux, if you're a Windows PC user, you're going to need to download the win32 disc imager. Once you've installed it, you need to run it and tell it where the operating system image file is located on your hard drive and what drive letter to write the image to for your SD card.

When choosing the actual drive letter that points to your SD card, make sure that the SD card you're using is blank since everything inside it is going to be overwritten. Getting back to Linux and Mac, you want to open up a new shell or a terminal as it's called on the Mac, and then navigate to the folder where you downloaded your disk image. In most cases it would be in /Downloads/Raspberry Pi/Raspbian.

Again, keep in mind that you will be overwriting everything on the SD card that you're going to be using for this installation. So use a fresh card or one you don't mind overwriting. At this point, make sure you do not have your SD card reader plugged in yet. The reason for this is because we need to find out which device our SD card will be using.

In your terminal or shell, type "df" (without the quotes) and then press ENTER. Now you should see a list of devices and the folders where they are mounted. This should be any of your internal hard drives or external hard drives and so forth. Now is the time when you want to plug in your SD card into your reader and then plug the reader into an open USB port.

Just wait a few moments for the card to mount. This can take a few seconds. After a few seconds, use the "df" command again. You should now see something different; an item that's listed as either no-name or volume/untitled. On the side you should see something listed like dev/disk3s1 or on Linux it would be something similar to dev/sdb1 or sdc1 or something like that next to it.

Drive assignments may vary from user to user so just take which device is listed next to that volume carefully. You want to make sure that you're using the SD device and not one of your hard drives. DD is an unforgiving command and it will overwrite without prejudice and without asking you if you're sure about doing so. So just be very careful. We can't stress this enough. You don't want to overwrite your main hard drive.

Once you know the device that you're going to write to, remember or write it down. Like what we mentioned earlier, it should be something like dev/disk3s1 on a Mac or something similar to dev/sdc1 on Linux. We're going to change this a little bit since we actually want to write the disk image to the entire card not just a partition on the card, which is what we have mounted right now.

So what we need to do now is unmount the SD card's partition before we can write to the entire card. We don't want to eject the card, we just want to unmount it. On your Mac you can open up your Disk Utility. It's in the same folder as your terminal. You then have to select the volume under the SD card device and click "unmount." You can also do this from the terminal, but you'll need to be on the superuser account. So to use Disk Utility using a superuser or root account, you can type the command below:

    $ sudo diskutil unmount/dev/disk3s1

On Linux you would do a similar thing. You would type in the command below:

    $ sudo unmount /dev/sdc1

You can type the command above or whatever your device assignment happens to be. One thing to remember is that the sudo command will always ask you for the administrator password in order to be able to execute the command, regardless of whether you're using a Mac or a Linux system. Once the SD card's partition is unmounted, we're going to run DD with 3 arguments; "bs," "if," and "of." Those stand for block size, in file, and out file respectively. You'll run the command exactly as below:

```
$ dd bs=1m if=2015-12-24-jessy-raspbian.img of=/dev/sdc1
```

Looking at the command above, you're going to be putting a value for block size; specifically 1m which stands for 1 megabyte, for "if" you'll be putting the name of the image file, and "of" is the location where you stored the image file. Regarding the location of the image file, we're going to change that a little bit. For example, if your device is listed as /dev/disc3s1, you want to change the "of" argument to /dev/rdisk3s1.

This may be different depending on your system so changing this will make sure that you use the entire SD card and not just the partition. In Linux for example, the "of" value would probably be something like /dev/sdb1 or /dev/sdc1. In this case, the letter after the letters "sd" could be different depending on your system. So in order to write to the whole card, you just need to take away the number "1." You should have something similar to the one below:

```
$ dd bs=1m if=2015-12-24-jessy-raspbian.img of=/dev/sdb
```

So that's pretty much of it. Once you're confident that you have the correct arguments for the DD command, hit ENTER. You're going to wait a few minutes while the SD card is being written on. At this point, you won't see any output while this process is ongoing. It will probably take a few minutes so just be patient.

If you're on Linux and you get an error, you might need to change the "bs" value from 1m to 1M (capital M). For some reason the case of the letter matters to a Linux system. Once this has been completed, you should be back to a command prompt. And assuming everything worked properly, you will now have a bootable operating system on your SD card.

You are now ready to boot your Raspberry Pi for the first time and start configuring your system, which we will cover on the next chapter.

## *Chapter 4: Booting OpenELEC & Raspbian for the First Time On Your Pi*

In the last chapter, we installed the operating system on the SD card. Let's now go ahead and insert the SD card into the slot on the underside of the Raspberry Pi. Keep in mind that the metal contacts of the SD card should be facing the underside of the board. First, we'll need at least a keyboard, a mouse, and a monitor. Go ahead and plug the keyboard and mouse to any of the available USB ports. Second, go ahead and plug in the Ethernet CAT5 or CAT6 cable on the Ethernet port on the Pi. Make sure that the other end of the Ethernet cable is plugged into your router. Third, go ahead and plug in the HDMI cable for your monitor.

Do not forget to use an HDMI to DVI converter if you have a DVI monitor. Lastly, plug in the microUSB cable of the 5V power supply to the microUSB port on your Raspberry Pi. Once you have everything plugged in, you should see the LEDs on the board start to light up. You will also see that the boot cycle has now started on the monitor. Just wait for login prompt to appear once the boot process has finished.

### Logging In

Once you have the login prompt, you want to use the default username which is "pi", and the default password, which is "raspberry" in all lower case. Once you type those in and press ENTER, you're in.

To start the desktop interface just type "start x" and press ENTER. Most people should be pretty familiar with how this desktop works. It's very similar to most other modern GUI interfaces. Let's now take a look at some of the applications that are available to you once you've successfully started the desktop interface of your Raspberry Pi.

- Scratch – This is basically a programming teaching tool. It is very similar to Karel. If you've ever taken a programming class, they use Karel the robot to teach you basic programming concepts.

- Python – Python is basically a very versatile and robust programming

40

language. It is used by many programmers and companies to make web based applications.

- Midori – Midori is a lightweight web browser. It takes its roots from Mozilla Firefox.

- File Manager – The file manager is very similar to the Window file manager. It lets you see the different directories and storage media that's associated with your Raspberry Pi. It also lets you see the important files in your Raspberry Pi.

- Terminal – Since Raspbian is basically a derivative of Debian Linux, it's no surprise that it also has a terminal similar to Linux. It has the same functions as a Linux terminal. It can also run all the terminal commands that you can run in a Linux system.

Now that we've pretty much seen what the Raspbian operating system looks like, let's go on ahead and see what OpenELEC looks like in a Raspberry Pi. Go ahead and mount the image of OpenELEC onto your SD card. The mounting process for OpenELEC is pretty much the same as Raspbian. If you're still logged into Raspbian on your Raspberry Pi, you must log out and shut the Pi down.

You shut the Raspberry Pi down by using the "halt" command. Again, in order for this command to work, you have to be a superuser. So you need to type in the word "sudo," then put a space by pressing the spacebar, type in the word "halt," and then press ENTER.

After you press ENTER, the Raspberry Pi will initiate the shutdown process. Once finished, you can now switch to the SD card with the OpenELEC operating system. Once the card is inserted, you can start booting your Raspberry Pi with the OpenELEC operating system. As you can see, you can pretty quickly change out cards and be up and running with a different operating system pretty quickly.

Once you have OpenELEC up and running, go ahead and explore the different parts of the operating system, see the different programs it has, and find out what it can do. This is the perfect time to explore and learn what the Raspberry Pi and its operating system is all about.

## *Chapter 5: How to Get Around in the Raspberry Pi's Unix-based Command Line Interface*

In this chapter, we will be going through some of the more basic commands that you're going to need to know in the command line shell for getting around the Unix-based file system. If you're running Raspbian, you'll need to know some of the standard Unix commands. Like most systems in Linux or Unix, files are stored in directory hierarchies.

You can also call them folders if you want to feel more comfortable with that term. When you login, unless you have a custom setting, you will most likely begin in your home/username directory. For Raspbian, the default username that we've been logging in with is Pi. So your home directory is going to be /home/Pi.

Most users on the system, except for root, will have their home directory stored within /home. The main exception is the root user's folder, which is stored in /root. On your command prompt you will see your home directory represented as a tilde symbol "~", and you can use that to easily get back to your home folder anytime.

Moving forward, let's get into working with directories. The first thing you might want to know is where you are and what directory you are located in. The first command that we're going to start with is PWD. PWD stands for Print Working Directory, which tells you the current directory that you're located in at that moment. You'll find that most commands in Unix are abbreviations of the activity that they perform.

As you can see from the output after you typed in PWD and pressed ENTER, you're in /home/pi. If you want to change to another directory, you need to use the CD command. For example, if you want to go to the top level directory—also called the root, which is not to be confused with the root user home directory—you type in this command:

        $ cd /

cd / represents the main directory; and the slash that is used is a forward slash. Many people mistakenly use the term backslash when they really mean forward slash. We call the "/" a forward slash because we read from left to right. So a slash leaning to the right is in the forward direction.

Typing the aforementioned command and pressing ENTER will bring you to the top level directory. There is nothing above this top level directory. It only has subdirectories beneath it. With that being said, let's now take a moment to look at a few subdirectories beneath the main root directory.

The first one that we're going to look at is "etc." Etc stores many of the system's configuration files so get familiar with this folder. If you want to change configuration settings, you're going to come here often. To go to the etc subdirectory from the root directory, type in the command below:

$ cd /etc

Now let's take a look at what's inside etc. We do that using the "ls" command. Ls is short for list and it just lists directory contents. ls also have some options associated with it that allows the user to change the way the listing looks.

Let's go ahead and take a look at a few common options of ls:

- -a – lists all files including hidden files in the directory. Files beginning with a dot "." are considered hidden. So anything that you name with a dot preceding the file name will be hidden automatically, unless you use the -a option to list the files.

- -l – lists all the files lengthwise down the screen.

- -p – puts a forward slash after the directory, which is inside the current directory that you are viewing. This lets you easily distinguish directories from files.

- --color – this will give you a colorful directory listing. However, this

43

doesn't always work. This command works depending on the system and if you're logging in remotely.

You can also combine multiple options with a single dash. Look at the example below:

    $ ls -lap

Typing the command above will give you all the options that you've indicated together with the list command. Now, to go back a directory, you have two options. In this particular case we can either type cd / to take us back to the main root directory since that's where we started before going into etc, or we can type the command below:

    $ cd ..

That's "cd" followed by a space, and then two dots. This takes us back one directory. We also have another command below:

    $ cd ../..

This command takes us back two directories if you happen to be two subdirectories in. So if you're still in the "etc" directory, go back one directory. There are a number of other directories to familiarize with within the root directory. Below are some of those directories:

- /bin – this directory is for commands and binaries.

- /sbin – this is for system and administrator commands.

- /user – this is for user-related files. It also has its own /bin and /sbin subdirectories.

- /var – var stands for variable. The /var/log subdirectory is a common destination for users who troubleshoot problems whose log file end up here.

- /home – As what we discussed before, this is for the user directories.

- /mnt – mnt, which stands for Mount, is pretty much the mount point for any external drives, image files, or things like that.

- /dev – this is for devices that interface with the hardware.

- /lib – this is for programs and program libraries.

There a lot more, but this is just a quick rundown of the more common directories that you're likely to encounter and use.

So how do we add, remove, or modify files and directories? Well, to create a new directory, type in the command below:

$ mkdir directoryname

Mkdir stands for make directory. This should be followed by a space and then the name of the directory that you want to create. To remove that empty directory, just used the command below:

$ rmdir directoryname

Rmdir stands for remove directory. This should be also followed by a space and then the name of the directory that you want to remove. Keep in mind that using this command with a non-empty directory would result to an error. There's another option to remove a directory even though it contains files and subdirectories. However, it can be a little dangerous in the wrong hands if they don't know what they're doing.

So please use with caution whenever you utilize the below command:

$ rm -rf directoryname

The -r option after the remove command means to do the removing process recursively, which drills down into the subdirectories located within the directory you're trying to remove. The -f option stands for Force, which forces the process to go through. So executing this command basically tells the system that you know what you're doing.

The system will allow you to execute the command as long as you have permission to that file or directory. Again, use these options only if you really need to. There won't be any dialogue box, pop-up window, or anything like that to save you from making a mistake with this command.

For copying files and directories, you'll be using the CP command. Look at the example command below:

$ cp filename1 filename2

First type in the cp command, followed by a space, followed by the name of the file to copy from, followed by another space, and then lastly the name of the file to copy to. Note that filename 1 and filename 2 should be different. Also, keep in mind that you need to have root (sudo) access in order to successfully execute this file.

To rename or move a file without duplicating it, use the command below:

$ mv filename1 filename2

The above command will essentially move the contents of filename1 to filename2. You can also specify directories where files are located. For example, let's say you want to copy the contents of /etc/hosts to your home folder. For that you would use the below command:

$ cp /etc/hosts /home/pi

Type in the cp command, followed by a space, then followed by the file-path of the file that you want to copy, and then another space, and then followed lastly by the file-path of the location where you want to copy the file to.

To move or copy a directory and its subdirectories, you want to use the -r option, which is again a recursive option.

$ cp -r directory1 directory2

If you want to find out about any of these commands, you can use the MAN command. MAN stands for manual. If you want to find out more about the cp command for example, you just have to type the command below:

$ man cp

This will pull up all the information about the cp command and all the options associated with it. The same applies to the mv, rm, and so forth.

## *Chapter 6: Python Programming in Raspberry Pi*

In this chapter, we're going to look at the best programming language for the Raspberry Pi; Python. It is considered by many as a notably powerful and dynamic language that is used to develop numerous application domains. Most programmers compare Python to Perl, Java, Ruby, Tcl, or Scheme. This is why Python is the primary language the Raspberry Pi is designed to operate on.

Below are some of the key features of the Python programming language:

- Superb for programming veterans and also remain simple enough for beginners to understand.

- Excellent scalability. Python is excellent in small projects; even better for large scale ones.

- Extremely portable and is compatible across all platforms

- Hardware embeddable

- Elegant and simple to understand syntax and semantics

- Excellent stability

- Has a huge standard library of pre-built subroutines, codes, etc.

Moving forward, we'll discuss how to get a very simple python program working. In addition, we'll also discuss how to use the Graphical User Interface to code basic python programs. However, what this chapter won't tackle is the nitty-gritty of learning how to program in Python. Python object-oriented programming is a whole topic in itself and is therefore out of the scope of this book.

Python programming in the Raspberry Pi is similar to Python programming using a normal desktop or laptop computer. It's just that with the Raspberry Pi, you're programming in a very portable, cheap, but robust platform. To start programming with Python on your Raspberry Pi, you must first make sure that you've successfully installed the Raspbian operating system.

Using the desktop of your Raspbian OS, click on the Menu option on the taskbar. Clicking on menu allows you to see the sub-menus for Raspbian. Click on the "Programming" sub-menu. Once you do that, you'll be presented with different programming applications for Raspbian. One of those applications would be your Python Editor.

Python Editors vary depending on the version of Raspbian running in your Raspberry Pi. However, the most common Python IDE would be Stan's Python Editor or SPE. Click on that and you'll be presented with GUI (Graphical User Interface) for your Python IDE (Integrated Development Environment).

The main window of your Python IDE is where you'll type the source code of the program that you're developing. To start making our simple Python program, first create a folder on your Raspbian desktop where we will put our python script. Just right click on any empty space on your desktop and click "Create New Folder." Don't forget to give your new folder a name.

Now, let's go ahead and develop a simple "Hello World" program using Python. To do so, go to   the code editor window of your Python IDE and type in the following code:

```
1      print "Hello World"
```

After typing this code in your editor, save it by clicking on the "File" menu at the menu of your Python IDE and then click on "Save." You will have to give your python script a name. In this case, just type in the filename as HelloWorld.py and save it inside the new folder that you have created on your desktop. Take note that filenames should not contain any spaces and that it should have a .py extension. This is the file extension for all Python scripts.

After saving the file, run the program by clicking on the "run" button on the menu bar of your Python IDE. At this point, two things should happen depending on which Python IDE you're using. Some IDEs will pull up the terminal and display the output of the program from there, while other IDEs will have a status bar at the bottom where it will show you the output of the Python program that you just ran.

Regardless of whatever mode of output your IDE uses, it should display the words "Hello World." If you want to run your Python script from the terminal itself and not from the IDE, all you need to do is navigate to where your Python script is located first and run the script from there. To do this, type the command below:

```
$ cd /home/pi/Desktop/foldername
```

The "foldername" is the name of the folder that you have created on the desktop. Once you're there type the below command to display the contents of that folder:

```
$ ls -l
```

Now, you'll see your HelloWorld.py file. To run this just type in the below command:

```
$ python HelloWorld.py
```

The command above is basically telling the system to use the Python interpreter to open the HelloWorld.py file. Press ENTER and you'll see the output; "Hello World."

Congratulations, you've just made your first Python program in your Raspberry Pi.

## *Conclusion*

Thank you for purchasing and reading this book. We hope that we've taught you all the basic things that you need to know about your Raspberry Pi; how to set it up, how to install the operating system so that you'll be able to develop programs using it.

From here, developing more intricate programs using Python is just a matter of learning the nitty-gritty of the programming language itself. There are many online tutorials out there that you can go and see to get in-depth knowledge of Python programming. Python is a very versatile and stable programming language and using it to make your Pi do wondrous things is easy, as long as you have an advanced knowledge of the programming language itself.

Again, Thank you so much and we hope that you succeed in your quest for knowledge on the Python programming language and that you have fun in finding ingenious ways to use your Raspberry Pi.

www.ingramcontent.com/pod-product-compliance
Lightning Source LLC
Chambersburg PA
CBHW061043050326
40689CB00012B/2958